AMAZING DINOSAURS

3-D

By Nancy Honovich

SCHOLASTIC

an imprint of
SCHOLASTIC
www.scholastic.com

Published by Tangerine Press, an imprint of Scholastic Inc.,
557 Broadway, New York, NY 10012
Scholastic Canada Ltd., Markham, Ontario

Design by Rosanna Brockley
Editorial by Ben Grossblatt and Leah Jenness
Photo research by Kara Stokes and Katie del Rosario
Photo research assistance by David Lister
3-D anaglyph effects by Matthew Fisher and Bill Whitaker
Production coordination by Tom Miller
Managing editorial by Michael del Rosario

Produced by becker&mayer!
11120 NE 33rd Place, Suite 101
Bellevue, WA 98004
www.beckermayer.com

If you have questions or comments about this product, please visit www.beckermayer.com/
customerservice and click on Customer Service Request Form.

304892 6/12
Manufactured in Shenzhen, China
10 9 8 7 6 5 4 3 2 1
ISBN: 978-0-545-47960-8
12005
Complies with CPSIA

Dinosaurs were some of the most amazing creatures to ever walk the earth. Are you ready to meet some face-to-face? In these pages, you'll see dinosaurs in all shapes and sizes—as big as a blue whale and as small as a crow. Some were ferocious meat-eaters, and others ate only plants. Some of these dinosaurs sprinted on two legs, and others plodded along on four huge feet. Dinosaur fossils have been found all over the world, from Africa to North America. Now you can see these amazing dinosaurs in eye-popping 3-D!

Contents

The strong, stocky legs of Apatosaurus supported the dinosaur's weight, much like the pillars of a bridge.

APATOSAURUS
(ah-PAT-uh-SOR-us)

Heavyweight

Apatosaurus belonged to a group of plant-eating dinosaurs called sauropods. Sauropods were huge—and Apatosaurus was no exception. It may have weighed about 37 tons (34 t). That's as heavy as five adult elephants! Because of its massive size, Apatosaurus moved more slowly than most dinosaurs. You might think that would make Apatosaurus vulnerable to attack. But most predators were too intimidated to take on a dinosaur so large.

Frequent Feeder

Apatosaurus was a fast grower. By the time the dinosaur was 5 years old, it was already half its adult size. And by age 10, it was almost full grown. To support its growing body, Apatosaurus had to eat a lot of food. Some scientists speculate that it ate all day long.

Not Too Smart

Apatosaurus may have been a supersized dinosaur, but it wasn't very smart. Its tiny brain probably weighed less than an apple!

Like other plant-eating dinosaurs, Apatosaurus had peglike teeth. The dinosaur used its teeth like a rake to pull and gather leaves and other foliage from trees and bushes.

APATOSAURUS WAS ALMOST AS LONG AS A BLUE WHALE—THE WORLD'S LARGEST ANIMAL.

Apatosaurus Stats

Type of dinosaur: Sauropod

When it lived: Late Jurassic

What its name means: Deceptive lizard

Where it lived: North America

Length, nose to tail: About 75 feet (23 m)

Weight: 75,000 pounds (34 t)

Food: Plants such as conifers, ginkgos, moss

Special feature: Apatosaurus could crack its tail like a whip if threatened.

ARCHAEOPTERYX
(AR-kee-OP-ter-iks)

Bird or Dinosaur?

Was Archaeopteryx a bird or a dinosaur? Scientists have been studying this question for years. Archaeopteryx had feathers, wings, and a wishbone, much like modern birds. But its teeth, bony tail, and belly ribs were typical of dinosaurs. Recent findings also show that Archaeopteryx had a shallow snout—a characteristic of dinosaurs. It seems that the bird theory may be for the birds—and Archaeopteryx is *really* a dinosaur.

Clawed Fingers

Archaeopteryx had three clawed fingers at the end of each wing. Scientists debate what these claws were used for. Some studies suggest that the claws may have been used to grasp prey. Others indicate that Archaeopteryx used its claws to climb trees.

ARCHAEOPTERYX WAS ABOUT THE SIZE OF A CROW.

Feathery Find

Recently, scientists studied the fossil of an Archaeopteryx feather. They learned that the feather was black. In modern birds, black feathers contain tiny granules that help make them stronger than feathers of a different color. This helps support birds when they fly. Scientists believe black feathers may have done the same for Archaeopteryx.

Archaeopteryx Stats

Type of dinosaur: Theropod

When it lived: Middle to Late Jurassic

What its name means: Ancient wing

Where it lived: Germany

Length, nose to tail: 1.5 feet (0.5 m)

Weight: Up to 18 ounces (0.5 g)

Food: Insects

Special feature: Archaeopteryx had black feathers.

Most birds have a ridged sternum, or breastbone. But Archaeopteryx had a flat breastbone. So in spite of its feathers and wings, Archaeopteryx may not have flown as well as birds do.

Archaeopteryx was a small dinosaur that had feathers and wings.

Because of its long, light legs, Aucasaurus was a fast runner. Its speed made it easier for Aucasaurus to chase down its prey.

AUCASAURUS
(AW-cah-SOR-us)

A Dinosaur Mystery!

In 1999, scientists digging at a site in Argentina discovered the skeleton of a meat-eating dinosaur named Aucasaurus. The skeleton was nearly complete and in great condition. The only problem was that the skull was broken. What happened to the Aucasaurus? Scientists suspect the dinosaur was struck or bitten in the head by a predator and died as a result of its wound.

Nest Raider

As the scientists in Argentina continued to dig, they made another discovery. They found a nest of sauropod eggs (like the ones pictured) beneath the Aucasaurus skeleton. This shows that Aucasaurus may have been trying to steal—and eat—the eggs just before it died.

Stealing another dinosaur's eggs doesn't seem like a good idea. But these dinosaurs may have typically gotten away with it. Scientists suspect that Aucasaurus hunted in packs that could easily have overtaken a nesting dinosaur.

Tiny Arms

Like Tyrannosaurus rex, Aucasaurus had useless arms. Its arms were tiny compared to the rest of its body. And the arms couldn't bend at the elbows, so they remained straight at all times.

Aucasaurus Stats

Type of dinosaur: Theropod

When it lived: Late Cretaceous

What its name means: Auca lizard (after the area of Patagonia where Aucasaurus fossils were found)

Where it lived: Argentina

Length, nose to tail: 13 feet (4 m)

Weight: 1,500 pounds (700 kg)

Food: Meat, dinosaur eggs

Special feature: Aucasaurus had short, stumpy fingers, so it was unable to grasp prey.

AUCASAURUS WAS ABOUT AS LONG AS A SIBERIAN TIGER.

BRACHIOSAURUS
(BRACK-ee-uh-SOR-us)

Supersized Dinosaur

In 1900, Brachiosaurus fossils were discovered near the Colorado River. Scientists studying the fossils concluded that this plant-eating sauropod would have stood close to 50 feet (15 m) tall. That's taller than the Green Monster—the famous left-field wall in Boston's Fenway Park. Scientists were amazed by the size of Brachiosaurus and dubbed it one of the largest dinosaurs that ever lived.

Head above the Rest

Brachiosaurus had an advantage over smaller plant-eaters when it came to finding food. Because of its super-long neck, which measured 30 feet (9 m), Brachiosaurus could easily graze the tops of tall trees. The dinosaur would use its chisel-shaped teeth to pull off leaves and tough conifer needles, which it would swallow whole.

BRACHIOSAURUS WAS MORE THAN TWICE AS TALL AS A GIRAFFE, THE WORLD'S TALLEST ANIMAL.

Brachiosaurus swallowed its food without chewing. This would have meant food took a long time to digest. It's possible Brachiosaurus also swallowed stones called gastroliths, which would have helped break down the food for digestion.

Brachiosaurus Stats

Type of dinosaur: Sauropod

When it lived: Middle to Late Jurassic

What its name means: Arm lizard

Where it lived: North America and parts of Africa

Length, nose to tail: 85 feet (26 m)

Weight: Up to 176,000 pounds (79,832 kg)

Food: Plants such as conifers, cycads, and ginkgos

Special feature: Brachiosaurus had large nasal openings in its skull, which could suggest it had a strong sense of smell.

Water Dweller?

Many water-dwelling animals have nostrils on the tops of their snouts. When they take a dip, they submerge their bodies but keep their nostrils above water to breathe. Brachiosaurus had nostrils on top of its snout, too. This made scientists wonder if the dinosaur was a water-dweller. But it turns out Brachiosaurus may have had a difficult time moving around in the water.

Brachiosaurus was a giant dinosaur that ate about 400 pounds (180 kg) of food each day.

Although Camarasaurus looked a lot like other sauropods, its neck and tail were slightly shorter than those of most sauropods.

CAMARASAURUS
(kah-MARE-uh-SOR-us)

Flood Plains

Camarasaurus was a plant-eating dinosaur that lived in what is today North America. More than a thousand Camarasaurus bones have been found at Dinosaur National Monument in Utah, including a nearly complete skeleton of a 17-foot (5-m) juvenile. Dinosaur National Monument was prone to floods. During these floods, water would wash the remains of dead Camarasaurus—as well as those of other dinosaurs—onto a sandbank, where fossils would eventually form.

CAMARASAURUS WAS AS LONG AS A BUS.

On the Move

Camarasaurus was often on the move. During the summer, it left lowland areas in favor of highlands. At that time of the year, these areas were damp. That environment would have created plenty of plants for Camarasaurus to eat. During the winter, the dinosaur headed back to the lowlands.

No Need for Nests

Some dinosaurs, including Velociraptors, built nests to shelter their eggs. That wasn't the case for sauropods like Camarasaurus. Sauropods laid their eggs in a line on the ground—probably while walking. It's unlikely that they stuck around until the eggs hatched.

Camarasaurus Stats

Type of dinosaur: Sauropod

When it lived: Late Jurassic

What its name means: Chambered lizard

Where it lived: North America

Length, nose to tail: About 50 feet (15 m)

Weight: 44,000 pounds (20,000 kg)

Food: Plants

Special feature: Camarasaurus migrated 200 miles (300 km) twice every year.

Camarasaurus babies weren't necessarily abandoned. Fossils of these young dinosaurs, like the one pictured, have been discovered alongside adult remains. They were probably part of a family group or herd.

CARNOTAURUS
(CAR-nuh-TOR-us)

Horned Head

Carnotaurus belonged to a group of dinosaurs called theropods. Like most theropods, Carnotaurus ate meat and walked on two legs. But Carnotaurus had one unusual feature. It had bull-like horns above its eyes. These horns probably weren't very sharp, so they likely couldn't have been used to kill prey. Carnotaurus males may have used the horns to head-butt their rivals during courtship. Ouch!

Hunting Problems

Carnotaurus had a slender lower jaw and teeth that were more delicate than those of other meat-eaters. As a result, Carnotaurus may have had a hard time holding struggling prey. This has led some scientists to believe Carnotaurus was a scavenger, an animal that fed on prey that was already dead.

CARNOTAURUS WAS ABOUT THREE TIMES THE LENGTH OF A POLAR BEAR.

Speedy Runner

Recent findings show Carnotaurus was a speedy runner. It had a large, powerful tail muscle that was attached to its upper leg bones. When the dinosaur contracted, or tightened, this muscle, it pulled the leg backward. This allowed the dinosaur to run with great force.

Animals need flexible tails to make sharp turns. Because of Carnotaurus's large tail muscle and rigid tail bones, the dinosaur would have had trouble making quick turns.

Carnotaurus Stats

Type of dinosaur: Theropod

When it lived: Middle Cretaceous

What its name means: Flesh-eating bull

Where it lived: South America

Length, nose to tail: 25 feet (8 m)

Weight: 3,300 pounds (1,500 kg)

Food: Meat

Special feature: Some scientists say Carnotaurus used its upper jaw like a club.

Carnotaurus's skin was covered in bumpy scales arranged in rows along its back and sides.

Scientists used to think dinosaurs such as Ceratosaurus dragged their tails on the ground. But now they know the tails were held above the ground.

CERATOSAURUS
(sih-RAT-uh-SOR-us)

Horned Nose

This meat-eating predator, which lived about 145 million years ago, had a bladelike horn over its snout. In spite of its lethal-looking appearance, the nose horn wasn't very dangerous. In addition, Ceratosaurus had hornlets, or bony ridges, above each eye. Scientists still aren't sure how these hornlets were used.

Crocodile Tail

Most experts agree that, although Ceratosaurus lived on land, it was also adapted for life in the water. Why? The dinosaur had a long, flexible tail that resembled that of a crocodile. It could easily have used its tail to propel itself through the water.

Sharp Teeth

Ceratosaurus had long, curved teeth, which it used to eat prey. These teeth were constantly replaced during the course of the dinosaur's life. Old, dull teeth fell out to make way for new, sharp teeth.

The ability to swim allowed Ceratosaurus to hunt in the water as well as on the land. In fact, Ceratosaurus fossils have been found alongside the remains of crocodiles, giant fish, and other water-dwelling creatures it may have preyed on.

Ceratosaurus Stats

Type of dinosaur: Theropod

When it lived: Late Jurassic

What its name means: Horn lizard

Where it lived: North America and parts of Africa

Length, nose to tail: Up to 20 feet (6 m)

Weight: 2,000 pounds (900 kg)

Food: Sauropods and large fish

Special feature: Ceratosaurus had large eyes, so its vision was probably very good.

CERATOSAURUS WAS ABOUT AS LONG AS A SALTWATER CROCODILE.

COMPSOGNATHUS
(comp-sog-NAY-thus)

Striking Jaw

Only two Compsognathus skeletons have been discovered so far, but both are well preserved. The fossils reveal that Compsognathus had an unusual jaw. The upper part was made of bone struts that neatly interlocked. These bone struts fit on a shallow lower jaw. Scientists thought the jaw was so striking that they named the dinosaur after it. The word *compsognathus* comes from Latin terms meaning "pretty jaw."

Small but Fast

Compsognathus was a fast runner. It could reach speeds of up to 40 mph (64 kph). That's about the speed of an ostrich, the fastest two-legged animal today. Compsognathus could reach such speeds because it had slim legs and large feet. Also, its bones were hollow, so it didn't have extra weight slowing it down.

COMPSOGNATHUS WAS ABOUT THE LENGTH OF A TURKEY.

A long tail helped Compsognathus get around. It kept the dinosaur from tipping forward. It also kept Compsognathus stable as it made sharp turns.

Feathers or Skin?

Was Compsognathus a feathered dinosaur? Scientists aren't sure. Relatives of Compsognathus—including Sinosauropteryx—have been discovered with feathers that covered their bodies like fur. However, so far, no Compsognathus fossils discovered have shown evidence of feathers. But the fossils do reveal that Compsognathus had bumpy skin.

Compsognathus Stats

Type of dinosaur: Theropod

When it lived: Late Jurassic

What its name means: Pretty jaw

Where it lived: Germany and France

Length, nose to tail: About 4 feet (1.2 m)

Weight: Up to 8 pounds (4 kg)

Food: Lizards, insects, small mammals

Special feature: Sharp claws on each hand could have helped Compsognathus grasp prey.

Compsognathus was a small dinosaur with a pointed head and sharp teeth.

Dicraeosaurus's long neck and tail helped the dinosaur keep its balance as it walked.

DICRAEOSAURUS
(di-CRAY-uh-SOR-us)

Family Features

Dicraeosaurus was a sauropod that belonged to a family of dinosaurs called diplodocids. These massive dinosaurs had long necks and tails but short legs. The rear legs were longer than the front legs. This made the dinosaur's head and neck appear as if they were angled slightly downward. Dicraeosaurus looked like a typical diplodocid except that its neck was thicker and its tail a bit shorter than most.

DICRAEOSAURUS WAS ABOUT AS LONG AS A SCHOOL BUS.

Spiny Back

Dicraeosaurus means "double-forked lizard." This refers to the bony spines along the dinosaur's neck and upper back. These spines, which grew from the backbone, were not straight. Instead, they were Y-shaped, like a double-pronged fork.

It isn't clear how Dicraeosaurus used its spines. One idea is that the spines made the dinosaur appear fierce and discouraged enemies from attacking.

Other Plant-eaters

Dicraeosaurus fossils were discovered in the African country of Tanzania. Other plant-eating dinosaurs discovered in this area include Giraffatitan and Kentrosaurus. These three dinosaurs were different sizes. That means they would have eaten plants that grew at different heights. So they probably didn't need to compete at mealtime.

Dicraeosaurus Stats

Type of dinosaur: Sauropod

When it lived: Late Jurassic

What its name means: Double-forked lizard

Where it lived: Central Africa (Tanzania)

Length, nose to tail: 45 feet (14 m)

Weight: 20,000 pounds (9,000 kg)

Food: Conifers and other plants

Special feature: Dicraeosaurus had small nostrils above its snout, which it used to breathe.

DIPLODOCUS
(dip-LOD-uh-cuss)

A Giant among Giants

Diplodocus was one of the largest animals to ever walk upon the earth. It had a long neck and a long, whiplike tail. These enormous plant-eaters weighed 16 tons (14.5 t) and grew longer than four school buses parked end to end. Sauropod dinosaurs like Diplodocus weighed 15 times as much as the heaviest four-legged animal today.

Tale of the Neck

It used to be thought that Diplodocus and other sauropods held their heads up high. But over the years computer models suggested that the dinosaurs held their necks out straight. More recent computer models showed that Diplodocus usually held its neck at a 45-degree angle, halfway between vertical and straight forward.

AN ELEPHANT WOULD HAVE LOOKED VERY SMALL NEXT TO DIPLODOCUS.

Supersonic *CRACK!*

Sauropods had enormous tails that tapered to thin tips. Did they use their tails like whips to defend themselves, or did these giants use them to produce a loud "crack" to scare predators and communicate with fellow sauropods? No one knows for sure.

> The cracking sound of a whip is the shock wave caused by the thin tip going faster than the speed of sound for one moment.

Diplodocus Stats

Type of dinosaur: Sauropod

When it lived: Late Jurassic

What its name means: Double-beam

Where it lived: North America

Length, nose to tail: 177 feet (54 m)

Weight: About 16 tons (14.5 t)

Food: Conifer trees, ginkgos, horsetails, ferns, and bushes

Special feature: Diplodocus may have whipped its long tail at supersonic speeds.

Like a construction crane, Diplodocus's heavy body worked as a counterweight to its long neck. This kept the dinosaur from toppling over.

Gigantoraptor was similar to birds today. It had a toothless beak and may have had feathers on parts of its body.

GIGANTORAPTOR
(jeye-GAN-toh-RAP-tor)

A Big Surprise

Oviraptorosaurs were a group of birdlike dinosaurs with small heads and beaks. For years, scientists believed these dinosaurs were little, weighing about 88 pounds (40 kg). But in 2005, they got a big surprise. They discovered a new species of oviraptorosaur that was about 35 times as heavy! They named it Gigantoraptor.

Dinosaurs of a Feather

There was no trace of feathers among Gigantoraptor fossils that scientists discovered, but that doesn't mean this dinosaur didn't have plumes. Other oviraptorosaurs had feathers, so it's possible Gigantoraptor did, too. If that's true, scientists believe that the feathers may have been used to attract a mate during courtship.

GIGANTORAPTOR WAS ALMOST THREE TIMES AS TALL AS AN ADULT HUMAN.

Bad Reputation

Oviraptorosaurs—like Gigantoraptor—once had a reputation for being egg-eaters. Years ago, scientists discovered the fossil of an oviraptorosaur lying over a nest of eggs. At first, they believed the dinosaur was trying to steal the eggs for dinner. But it turns out the oviraptorosaur was caring for its own eggs.

We don't know if Gigantoraptor ate eggs, but scientists believe it was omnivorous, eating both plants and meat.

Gigantoraptor Stats

Type of dinosaur: Theropod

When it lived: Late Cretaceous

What its name means: Gigantic thief

Where it lived: Northern China

Length, nose to tail: 26 feet (8 m)

Weight: 3,000 pounds (1,400 kg)

Food: Plants and meat

Special feature: Gigantoraptor was a fast grower.

KENTROSAURUS
(KEN-truh-SOR-us)

Out of Africa

Kentrosaurus was a plant-eating dinosaur that lived during the late Jurassic period. Kentrosaurus belonged to a group of dinosaurs called stegosaurs, known for their spikes and the bony plates that ran along their backs. Most stegosaurs lived in North America or China. But Kentrosaurus lived in eastern Africa. More than 1,200 Kentrosaurus bones have been discovered in this region!

Chomp!

Like other stegosaurs, Kentrosaurus used its ridged teeth to eat plants. Because its front legs were shorter than its hind legs, it usually kept its head near the ground, chomping up ferns and other low-lying foliage. Some scientists believe the dinosaur could also reach higher-growing plants by rearing up on its hind legs.

KENTROSAURUS WAS ALMOST TWICE THE LENGTH OF A COW.

Heavy Hitter

Kentrosaurus had a powerful weapon to defend itself with against predators: a long, flexible tail lined with two rows of spikes. If an enemy got too close, Kentrosaurus would whip its tail with bone-shattering force.

Kentrosaurus also had bony plates sticking up from its back and shoulders. These plates wouldn't have been as dangerous as its spiky tail, but they may have given the dinosaur some protection from predators.

Kentrosaurus Stats

Type of dinosaur: Stegosaur

When it lived: Late Jurassic

What its name means: Spiked lizard

Where it lived: Africa

Length, nose to tail: 15 feet (4.5 m)

Weight: Up to 4,000 pounds (1,800 kg)

Food: Plants, such as ferns, and fruit from nonflowering plants

Special feature: Kentrosaurus had a strong sense of smell.

Kentrosaurus had spikes that measured up to 2 feet (60 cm) long.

Microraptor probably used the wings on its forelegs and hind legs to glide across the sky from tree to tree.

MICRORAPTOR
(MY-crow-RAP-tor)

A Link to Birds?

In 2002, scientists discovered one of the smallest dinosaurs known. Microraptor was only 3 feet (1 m) long from beak to tail. But that wasn't the only interesting thing about this dinosaur. Microraptor had long feathers similar to those of modern birds that fly. In fact, many scientists believe that Microraptor may hold clues to how dinosaurs evolved into birds.

What a Trip!

Microraptor probably wasn't able to run or walk across the ground. Why? Its hind-leg feathers were long. Microraptor would have tripped over them with each step it took! So when Microraptor wasn't airborne, it perched in trees.

On the Hunt

To avoid damaging its feathers, Microraptor had to keep its wings pulled back or lifted. So it probably would have been hard for the dinosaur to use its claws to reach down and grab prey. Instead, Microraptor likely snagged a meal with its beak and then swallowed it whole.

Microraptor soared through the sky but didn't flap its wings like most birds do today. Instead, it glided from one tree branch to another, like a flying squirrel, using its tail feathers to stay stable along the way.

Microraptor Stats

Type of dinosaur: Theropod

When it lived: Early Cretaceous

What its name means: Small thief

Where it lived: Asia (China)

Length, nose to tail: About 3 feet (1 m)

Weight: 2 pounds (1 kg)

Food: Meat

Special feature: Microraptor could see well in the dark, so it may have hunted at night.

MICRORAPTOR WAS ABOUT THE SIZE OF A DUCK.

MONOLOPHOSAURUS
(mah-no-LOAF-oh-SOR-us)

A Different World

Earth's continents were once joined together as a supercontinent named Pangaea. But about 180 million years ago, the continents began to drift away from one another. As this happened, their climates changed. Areas that had once been hot and dry suddenly became warm and lush—perfect conditions for plants and animals. The area known today as China was just one region that experienced such a change. Many dinosaurs evolved here during this time—including a meat-eater named Monolophosaurus.

Crowning Glory

Monolophosaurus—whose name means "single-crested lizard"—is best known for the crest on its head. The crest was formed by bony ridges that extended from the dinosaur's snout to the area between its eyes. In spite of its bony exterior, the crest was hollow.

MONOLOPHOSAURUS WAS MORE THAN TWICE AS LONG AS A GRIZZLY BEAR.

Because Monolophosaurus's crest was hollow, it wouldn't have been very sturdy. So it's unlikely the dinosaur used it to head-butt enemies. Instead, the crest was probably used to attract mates.

What's in a Name?

Think the word *Monolophosaurus* is a mouthful? When the dinosaur was discovered in 1987, news reports called it a *Jiangjunmiaosaurus*. That word comes from a Chinese phrase that means "old desert inn," referring to an inn near the discovery site. Scientists eventually combined parts of both words to create the dinosaur's full name: *Monolophosaurus jiangji*.

Monolophosaurus Stats

Type of dinosaur: Theropod

When it lived: Middle Jurassic

What its name means: Single-crested lizard

Where it lived: Asia (China)

Length, nose to tail: 16 feet (5 m)

Weight: About 1,000 pounds (475 kg)

Food: Meat

Special feature: Monolophosaurus likely had sharp teeth, which it used to tear into prey.

Monolophosaurus was a crested meat-eater that may have
lived near lakes or rivers in the area that is now China.

Parasaurolophus had a bony crest on its head that measured more than 3 feet (1 m) long.

PARASAUROLOPHUS
(par-ah-SOR-OHL-oh-fus)

Ducklike Beak

Parasaurolophus belonged to a family of dinosaurs called hadrosaurids. Different hadrosaurids had different characteristics. Some, like Parasaurolophus, had crests on top of their heads. Others were known for their large, bulky size. So what did these family members have in common? They all had ducklike beaks, which they used to pluck—and eat—leafy greens.

Mixed Movements

Another common feature of hadrosaurids was their ability to walk on either two legs or four. For example, when Parasaurolophus foraged for food, it used all four legs. But when it ran, it used only its two hind legs.

PARASAUROLOPHUS WAS ABOUT AS LONG AS A LARGE RV.

Noisemaker

Parasaurolophus's long, bony crest swept back past its head. Long tubes inside the crest were attached to its nose. Parasaurolophus may have used these tubes to make a sound—kind of like the way an elephant trumpets through its trunk.

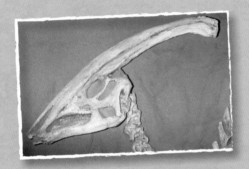

Why would Parasaurolophus make such sounds? The noises may have been a way to attract mates—or a warning signal to tell other dinosaurs, "Hey, guys! Look out for that predator!"

Parasaurolophus Stats

Type of dinosaur: Ornithopod

When it lived: Late Cretaceous

What its name means: Beside crested lizard

Where it lived: North America

Length, nose to tail: 31 feet (9 m)

Weight: 5,600 pounds (2,540 kg)

Food: Plants, possibly leaves, pine needles, and twigs

Special feature: Parasaurolophus was probably a fast runner.

PSITTACOSAURUS
(SIT-uh-koh-SOR-us)

Parrot Beak

It's no wonder Psittacosaurus's name means "parrot lizard." This dinosaur's curved beak looked a lot like the beaks you see on parrots today. Psittacosaurus's beak was made of a bony center covered in keratin—the same material that makes up human fingernails. This would have made its beak extra strong and sharp—perfect for snipping tough leaves and cones, like those found on cycads, a type of tree.

Super Swimmer

If Psittacosaurus did take an occasional dip in the lake, it might have been a great swimmer. Its long, crocodile-like tail was one-third of the dinosaur's length. Psittacosaurus may have used the tail to propel itself forward while paddling with its legs.

PSITTACOSAURUS WAS BIGGER THAN A GAZELLE.

Psittacosaurus was not limited to life in the water. It had powerful hind legs and a light skeleton. These features would have made Psittacosaurus a fast runner.

Features

Psittacosaurus belonged to a group of dinosaurs called ceratopsians, which were known for their curved beaks. But ceratopsians also had other features not shared by the Psittacosaurus. These included neck horns and a frill—like the one sported by the group's most famous member: Triceratops.

Psittacosaurus Stats

Type of dinosaur: Ceratopsian

When it lived: Early Cretaceous

What its name means: Parrot lizard

Where it lived: Asia

Length, nose to tail: About 6 feet (2 m)

Weight: About 88 pounds (40 kg)

Food: Plants, such as cycads

Special feature: Some Psittacosaurus species had quills on their tails.

Many Psittacosaurus fossils have been found in an area that was once a lake. So it's possible that Psittacosaurus spent part of its time in water.

Pteranodon had enormous wings. When outstretched, they spanned about 27 feet (7 m) from tip to tip.

PTERANODON
(ter-RAN-uh-dahn)

Not a Dino!

So did you think Pteranodon was a dinosaur? It's not! It's actually a type of winged reptile called a pterosaur. Pterosaurs like Pteranodon were the earliest known vertebrates—or animals with a backbone—that could fly. During the Late Cretaceous period, they soared across the sky—usually over the seaway that divided North America at the time.

Gone Fishing

Pteranodon would have spent much of its time searching for food as it flew over the seaway. When it spotted a fish, like the fossilized one pictured, it would swoop down and snatch the prey with its jaws. Because Pteranodon didn't have any teeth, it would have swallowed its meal whole.

Catching a Ride

Pteranodon was able to fly for hours without getting tired. How? The winged reptile would catch a ride on rising air currents called thermals. These currents would help lift Pteranodon, so it used as little energy as possible.

Pteranodons were similar to modern-day bats. They had three clawed fingers, as well as an elongated fourth finger that formed the structure of their wing.

PTERANODON'S WINGSPAN WAS ABOUT AS WIDE AS THAT OF A SMALL PLANE.

Pteranodon Stats

Type of dinosaur: It's not a dino! It's actually a flying reptile called a pterosaur.

When it lived: Late Cretaceous

What its name means: Winged and toothless

Where it lived: North America

Length: About 6 feet tall (1.8 m)

Weight: 40 pounds (18 kg)

Food: Fish and other marine creatures

Special feature: Pteranodon had a tall crest on top of its head, which it may have used to attract a mate.

SPINOSAURUS
(SPY-nuh-SOR-us)

Supersized Predator

Spinosaurus was one of the largest predators that ever lived. It measured about 50 feet (15 m) long. That's even bigger than T. rex! Size isn't the only thing Spinosaurus is known for. It had large, bony spines along its back and a long snout lined with razor-sharp teeth. It was one of the most intimidating-looking creatures of its time!

Fishy Fact

You might think that large, scary-looking Spinosaurus hunted creatures close to its own size. But this dinosaur preferred to eat fish. Spinosaurus would plunge its long, crocodile-like snout into the water to skewer large fish with its teeth.

SPINOSAURUS WAS AS LONG AS THE LARGEST HUMPBACK WHALE.

Spiny Sail

Spinosaurus had a structure called a sail that stood up on its back. This sail was made of long spines measuring up to 6 feet (2 m). These sail bones were part of the animal's vertebrae, or backbones.

Spinosaurus's sail may have helped control its body temperature, keeping it warm by collecting heat from the sun and helping it cool down by releasing heat when Spinosaurus was in the shade.

Spinosaurus Stats

Type of dinosaur: Theropod

When it lived: Middle Cretaceous

What its name means: Spiny lizard

Where it lived: Africa

Length, nose to tail: 50 feet (15 m)

Weight: About 8,000 pounds (3,629 kg)

Food: Fish, and possibly meat left over from other dinosaur kills

Special feature: Spinosaurus had large, sharp claws, which it may have used as weapons.

Spinosaurus was a giant meat-eater with a large sail on its back. The sail would have made this scary dinosaur even more intimidating to other animals.

Stegosaurus had two rows of bony plates, but the plates were too flimsy to be used for protection.

STEGOSAURUS
(steg-uh-SOR-us)

Colorful Plates

Stegosaurus was a plant-eating dinosaur that lived about 145 million years ago. It is best known for the 17 plates that were embedded in its back. Scientists believe these plates were colorful. The plates may have been used to attract mates, or they may have helped a Stegosaurus identify different dinosaurs of its species.

Busted Myth

Scientists once believed that its plates absorbed heat when Stegosaurus was in the sun. Blood vessels inside the plates would then carry the heat through the dinosaur's body to keep it warm. However, recent finds show that although the plates contained vessels, these tubes didn't lead anywhere—so they couldn't have actually warmed the body.

STEGOSAURUS WAS ABOUT THE LENGTH OF A STRETCH LIMO.

Telling Tails

Stegosaurus wasn't the smartest dinosaur around. Its brain was the size of a walnut. Scientists once believed that this little brain was too small for an animal of its size. So they suggested that the dinosaur had a second brain—at the base of its tail. However, this was later proved to be false.

Though its tail was not the source of Stegosaurus's intelligence, it did help the dinosaur defend itself. The tail contained long spikes that Stegosaurus could have used as a weapon against predators.

Stegosaurus Stats

Type of dinosaur: Stegosaur

When it lived: Late Jurassic

What its name means: Roof lizard

Where it lived: North America

Length, nose to tail: About 30 feet (9 m)

Weight: 6,800 pounds (3,084 kg)

Food: Plants, such as cycads, conifers, and ferns

Special feature: Stegosaurus was a poor chewer, so it may have swallowed stones called gastroliths to help grind its food for digestion.

SUCHOMIMUS
(SOOK-oh-MIME-us)

Dino-mite Discovery

In 1997, while scouting for dinosaurs in the Sahara Desert, a team of scientists came across a large claw lying on the surface of the sand. They immediately began to dig around the area, hoping to find more. Soon they had uncovered 400 bones. The bones all belonged to Suchomimus, a large dinosaur that had lived in Africa during the Middle Cretaceous period.

Sickle-shaped Claw

Suchomimus's thumb claw was long and shaped like a sickle. This suggests that Suchomimus may have used it to hook fish in the rivers that ran through this region of Africa more than 100 million years ago.

Toothy Snout

Suchomimus had a long, narrow snout that was lined with about 100 teeth. The teeth at the tip of the dinosaur's snout were the longest and may have also been used to spear fish. In fact, Suchomimus's snout and teeth are like those of the modern-day gharial, a type of crocodilian that feeds on fish.

SUCHOMIMUS WAS ABOUT TWICE AS LONG AS THE SALTWATER CROCODILE, THE LARGEST LIVING REPTILE IN THE WORLD TODAY.

Suchomimus was well adapted for fishing, but it may have been hard for it to find food. During its time, the area of Africa where it lived was filled with predators, such as giant crocodiles, which would have competed with Suchomimus for food.

Suchomimus Stats

Type of dinosaur: Theropod

When it lived: Middle Cretaceous

What its name means: Crocodile mimic

Where it lived: Africa

Length, nose to tail: 36 feet (11 m)

Weight: About 5,500 pounds (2,500 kg)

Food: Mainly fish

Special feature: Suchomimus had strong forelimbs, which would have helped the dinosaur seize and hold prey.

Suchomimus's name means "crocodile mimic." It is named for its snout, which looks like that of a crocodile.

Triceratops had three horns and a frill around its neck.
It may have used its horns and frill to defend itself.

TRICERATOPS
(try-SER-ah-tops)

Horns and Frills

Triceratops was a plant-eating ceratopsian that roamed parts of North America during the Late Cretaceous period. Triceratops had a neck frill and three horns on its head. The horns—which were common among many ceratopsians—gave it the appearance of a modern-day rhinoceros. Fossils from many Triceratops have been found together, suggesting this dinosaur traveled in herds.

Replacement Teeth

Triceratops's mouth was filled with rows of teeth. Beneath each tooth was a replacement tooth. When a tooth wore away, the replacement tooth grew in its place. Triceratops could lose hundreds of teeth throughout its life.

TRICERATOPS WAS ABOUT TWICE THE SIZE OF A RHINOCEROS.

Under Attack

Triceratops may have been a target for many large predators that lived in North America during its time. Bite marks have been discovered on some Triceratops bones. What could have been the culprit? Many signs point to T. rex.

No one's sure how Triceratops used its frill and horns. Some scientists say they were used for defense. The large frill may have protected the dinosaur's neck, and the horns may have been used to gore enemies.

Triceratops Stats

Type of dinosaur: Ceratopsian

When it lived: Late Cretaceous

What its name means: Three-horned face

Where it lived: North America

Length, nose to tail: About 29 feet (9 m)

Weight: 19,800 pounds (9,000 kg)

Food: Plants such as palms, cycads, and ferns

Special feature: Triceratops had a parrotlike beak, which it used to clip plants.

TYRANNOSAURUS REX

(tuh-RAN-us-SORE-us REKS)

Dangerous Dinosaur

There weren't many dinosaurs that could battle T. rex and survive. This giant meat-eater was the ultimate killing machine. It had a muscular build, sharp teeth, and powerful jaws that could crush bones. These features allowed T. rex to overpower dinosaurs that were twice its weight. It's no surprise this dinosaur's name means "tyrant lizard king."

Speedy Runner

Scientists once believed that T. rex wasn't a speedy runner. But new evidence suggests otherwise. T. rex had large, strong muscles in its tail that were attached to its upper leg bones. These muscles would have given T. rex a powerful stride as it sprinted for its prey.

T. REX WAS ABOUT TWICE AS LONG AS A GREAT WHITE SHARK.

Deadly Bite

T. rex was a fierce killer. It used its powerful neck muscles and knifelike teeth to tear into the flesh of its prey. Scientists estimate that T. rex could eat up to 500 pounds (230 kg) of food in one bite!

Believe it or not, scientists have discovered T. rex droppings! These droppings—or coprolites—contain parts of the dinosaur's meal. So what was on T. rex's menu? A Triceratops!

T. Rex Stats

Type of dinosaur: Theropod

When it lived: Late Cretaceous

What its name means: Tyrant lizard king

Where it lived: North America

Length, nose to tail: 40 feet (12 m)

Weight: 14,000 pounds (6,350 kg)

Food: Dinosaurs, mammals, lizards

Special feature: T. rex's eyes faced forward, which allowed the dinosaur to see objects that were in front of it very clearly.

Tyrannosaurus rex had supersized teeth. Some of its teeth were as long as bananas!

DINO TIME LINE

Dinosaurs lived during a time in history called the Mesozoic Era, which began **250** *million* years ago! The Mesozoic Era is subdivided into three periods: the Triassic Period (250–201 million years ago), the Jurassic Period (200–146 million years ago), and the Cretaceous Period (145–65 million years ago). This Dino Time Line shows when the dinosaurs in this book lived.

Jurassic Period: 200–146 Million Years Ago

Middle Jurassic **Middle to Late Jurassic** **Late Jurassic**

| Monolophosaurus | Archaeopteryx | Brachiosaurus | Apatosaurus | Camarasaurus | Ceratosaurus | Compsognathus | Dicraeosaurus | Diplodocus | Kentrosaurus | Stegosaurus |

Cretaceous Period: 145–65 Million Years Ago

Early Cretaceous **Late Cretaceous**

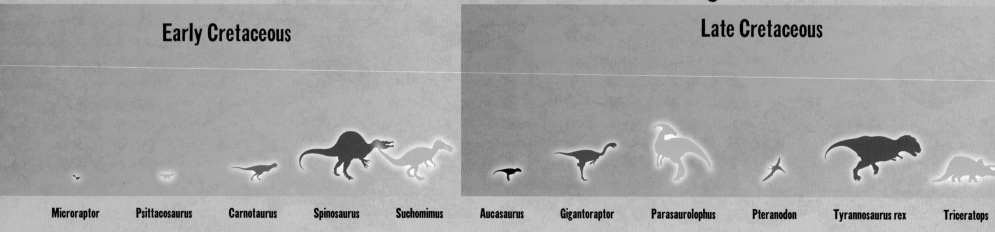

| Microraptor | Psittacosaurus | Carnotaurus | Spinosaurus | Suchomimus | Aucasaurus | Gigantoraptor | Parasaurolophus | Pteranodon | Tyrannosaurus rex | Triceratops |